Deer

Julie Murray

Abdo
EVERYDAY ANIMALS
Kids

abdopublishing.com

Published by Abdo Kids, a division of ABDO, PO Box 398166, Minneapolis, Minnesota 55439.
Copyright © 2016 by Abdo Consulting Group, Inc. International copyrights reserved in all countries.
No part of this book may be reproduced in any form without written permission from the publisher.

Printed in the United States of America, North Mankato, Minnesota.

102015

012016

Photo Credits: iStock, Shutterstock

Production Contributors: Teddy Borth, Jennie Forsberg, Grace Hansen

Design Contributors: Candice Keimig, Dorothy Toth

Library of Congress Control Number: 2015941766

Cataloging-in-Publication Data

Murray, Julie.

 Deer / Julie Murray.

   p. cm. -- (Everyday animals)

ISBN 978-1-68080-114-9 (lib. bdg.)

Includes index.

1. Deer bison--Juvenile literature.   I. Title.

599.65--dc23

                    2015941766

Table of Contents

Deer

Deer come in all sizes. Some are big. Some are small.

Most deer are brown or gray.

Others are reddish in color.

Deer have good eyesight. They can smell and hear well, too!

Male deer are called bucks.

They have antlers. They shed

their antlers in spring.

A female is a doe. A baby is a fawn. Some fawns have white spots.

buck

doe

fawn

13

Deer eat only plants.

They like leaves and grass.

Deer live in forests. They live in mountains. They also live in grassy fields.

Deer can run fast.

They can jump high, too!

496

Have you seen a deer?

Features of a Deer

antlers (male)

hooves

ears

tail

Glossary

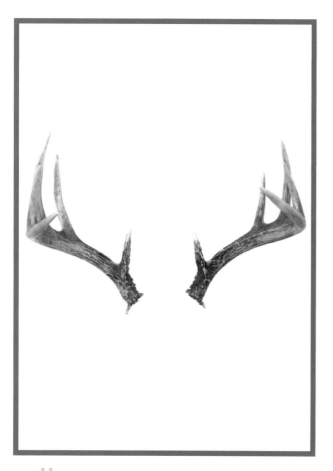

antlers
solid branched horns of an animal of the deer family.

shed
to lose as part of a normal process.

Index

abdokids.com

Use this code to log on to abdokids.com and access crafts, games, videos, and more!

Abdo Kids Code:
EDK1149